W9-CIK-314

BE A MAKER!

Maker Projects for Kids Who Love
WOODWORKING

SARAH LEVETE

Crabtree Publishing Company
www.crabtreebooks.com

Crabtree Publishing Company

www.crabtreebooks.com

Author: Sarah Levete

Series Research and Development: Reagan Miller

Editors: Sarah Eason, Harriet McGregor,
   Tim Cooke, and Philip Gebhardt

Proofreaders: Claudia Martin, Wendy Scavuzzo,
   and Petrice Custance

Editorial director: Kathy Middleton

Design: Paul Myerscough

Cover design: Paul Myerscough

Photo research: Rachel Blount

**Production coordinator and
   Prepress technician:** Tammy McGarr

Print coordinator: Katherine Berti

Consultant: Jennifer Turliuk, Bachelor of Commerce,
Singularity University Graduate Studies Program at
NASA Ames, Former President of MakerKids

Production coordinated by Calcium Creative

Photo Credits:

t=Top, bl=Bottom Left, br=Bottom Right

Kon-Tiki2 Expedition: p. 22; Shutterstock: 30gorkor: p. 15; Ben Bryant:
p. 11; Ermess: p. 27; G-stockstudio: p. 10; Kalcutta: p. 26; Robert Mandel:
p. 23; Monkey Business Images: p. 21; Optimarc: p. 7; Pi-Lens: pp. 1, 20;
Dr. Morley Read: p. 9; Vlad Romensky: p. 6; TFoxFoto: p. 14; Tantrik71:
p. 24; Sandra van der Steen: p. 25; Robert Wydro Studio: p. 4; Zeljka:
p. 16; Leonard Zhukovsky: p. 8; Tudor Photography: pp. 5, 12–13, 18–19,
28–29; Wikimedia Commons: Nandagopalrl: p. 17.

Cover: Tudor Photography

CONTENTS

TIME TO MAKE!

Take a piece of wood and fashion it into something useful or beautiful, or both. Wood is an amazing material that can be endlessly reused. In this book, we look at ways to use woodworking skills, from using popsicle sticks to making a birdhouse.

MAKER MOVEMENT

The maker movement is all about learning through hands-on, real-world experience. Working with wood is part of the maker movement. A makerspace is a place where people can gather to share resources, knowledge, and work on projects. Try new things and create new possibilities. Use your imagination, practical skills, and spirit of adventure to become a woodworker.

NEW FROM OLD

Become part of a centuries-old tradition of craftspeople who have enjoyed the process of **carpentry** to make best use of wood. At its most basic, wood can be used for strength in providing support in **construction**. It can also be shaped into simple or elaborate furniture.

Wood comes from a living tree. When part of a tree is cut down, the wood is no longer living. However, you can make it live by reshaping and forming it into something new. Treat it with wonder. Marvel at its structure and **properties**. Create and make something new.

Woodworking helps you to develop both your practical and creative skills.

4

WHAT DO YOU NEED?

All you need is a willingness to try, and to learn as you work. You will also need to follow safety guidelines. You will need pieces of wood and some basic tools. You do not need to buy new wood. Be a true maker and source material from **recycled** and discarded wood. Work with friends to share your skills and ideas. If something does not go according to plan, rethink it. Learn through experimentation—mistakes often lead to exciting new ideas. Use your creativity as you design. Use your math skills when measuring. Use your scientific understanding and wonder as you appreciate this extraordinary natural material.

SAFETY

Wood is a strong material. To shape or cut it, you need sharp tools. Observe the safety guidelines (see page 10) whenever you work with wood. It is essential to use such tools only when a responsible adult is supervising. Always remember to wash your hands after collecting wood.

Working on wood projects is a great team activity. You get to share your ideas and skills.

WOOD IN THE WORLD

All the wood people use for making objects comes from trees. When you work with wood, it helps to understand the source of this wonderful material. If you appreciate and understand the amazing strength and value of trees, you will better appreciate the remarkable material that you are working with.

TREE TIME

The trunk of a tree supports its weight. The bark is made from **cells** that have died. The bark acts as a barrier to protect the tree from insects and disease. Cells divide at the tips of twigs causing them to grow. Under the bark, layers of cells called the cambium divide, producing new tissue and widening the trunk. As the weather turns colder, the cells rest until the warmer weather returns. This cycle creates growth rings inside the trunk.

Look closely at the rings inside a tree trunk to find out more about the tree's age.

WOODY DIFFERENCES

There are more than 23,000 types of tree around the world. You do not need to be a tree specialist to be creative with woodwork, but it helps to know about the material you are working with. **Softwood** comes from **coniferous** trees such as cedar, fir, and pine. These trees, also known as evergreens, keep their leaves or needles all year round. Wood from **deciduous** trees is known as **hardwood**. These trees lose their leaves each fall. The wood from deciduous trees is usually **denser** than wood from coniferous trees, so it is stronger, but harder to work with. Baseball bats are made of hardwood.

Balsa wood is perfect for making light models such as airplanes. They fly, too!

WOODY MATTERS

The unique, or special, natural properties of wood make it useful and **versatile**. Wood is strong and heavy. It floats, does not **conduct** electricity, and is a good **insulator**. It is also long-lasting. Consider the wooden items you use at home and in school. What properties of wood make this material suitable for the purpose? Are there other properties that make wood special?

Be a Maker!

Go to your local park, woodland, or backyard. Select some sticks and pieces of bark. Find out which type of tree this wood comes from. Peel off the bark. What do you see inside? Talk with friends about the different ways you could use this wood. What happens when you bend a stick in one direction, then in the opposite direction? How do you think the characteristics of the wood could be used in construction?

WOOD UP CLOSE

Woodworking is nearly as old as trees! From wooden tools to wooden sculptures, humans have been working with wood for thousands of years. Early humans used stone tools to cut and carve wood. They burned wood for warmth, but they also used it to create **functional** and decorative objects.

A MATTER OF STRENGTH

The strength of wood makes it ideal for use in walls and roofs. It is used to make furniture that lasts for hundreds of years. Hardwoods, such as maple and walnut, take longer to grow than softwoods, so they are more expensive to produce. Look at a piece of bare, unfinished wood. The lines you see are the **grain**. Sometimes, you will notice irregular shapes in the grain. These are known as **knots** and mark where a branch has grown out from the trunk of a tree.

This carved wooden sculpture demonstrates the creative possibilities of working with wood.

8

BUG ALERT!

When trees are alive and rooted, they are the natural home to insects and bacteria. When wood is cut from a tree, it is still attractive to some bugs and pests. When workers delivered new **timber** to the Statue of Liberty, they delivered wood-eating bugs called termites, too. The termites made their home in the museum underneath the island monument. To prevent the critters from destroying the wooden museum, scientists coated paper towels with insecticide, a poison to get rid of the bugs. The hungry termites left their home to search for food and took the deadly insecticide back to their nest.

These termites love to chew through wood. Great for the termites—but bad news for the wood!

Be a Maker!

Compare objects made from a variety of materials, including wood. Touch them, smell them, look at their color. Ask your friends which materials appeal the most to them and why. Think about the properties of a material that you would create for modern-day needs. Can you create a material that fulfills all the functions of wood, and also has its beauty and form? Work with your friends to design a material that may be better suited to our needs than wood. How is this new material different from wood?

WORKING WOOD

Cutting or shaping wood requires very sharp tools, so woodworkers have to take care. Whenever you work with wood, it is essential to observe safety rules.

KEY SAFETY RULES

- Always work under the supervision of a responsible adult.
- Always wear goggles and a mask—when you cut wood, it can splinter, fly out, and harm your eyes.
- Always ask an experienced adult to teach you how to safely and correctly use tools such as saws, hammers, drills, and pliers.
- Wear gloves to protect your hands from splinters when you pick up or move wood.
- Do not wear long, loose sleeves, or jewelry that could get caught.
- Long hair should be tied back and held firmly under a hat.
- Safely store tools such as saws and hammers.
- Keep the working area clear, and clean up sawdust.
- Whenever you build a wooden structure, ask a responsible adult to check that it is safe to use.
- If you get a splinter, ask an adult for assistance in removing it.

Measure carefully before you start cutting. Then recheck your measurement. Once you have cut a piece of wood, you cannot make it longer again!

MARKING AND FIXING

Measure twice and cut once! Remember that phrase and you will avoid cutting too short. Use a measuring tape, ruler, and pencil. To attach pieces of wood together, use wood glue, a hammer and nails, or a screwdriver and screws. Nails have flat heads so they leave a smooth finish when hammered in. If you use screws, you must drill a hole first. This uses less force than inserting a nail, which means there is less risk of splitting the wood. A **claw hammer** is useful if you need to remove nails from pieces of wood. Sandpaper smoothes rough wood, and takes off paint or varnish. This is useful when you are refashioning wooden items.

The Todai-ji Temple in Nara, Japan, is one of the largest wooden structures in the world. It is more than 1,200 years old.

Be a Maker!

Colonial Americans, Japanese woodworkers, and the ancient Chinese developed ways to fasten wood using only the wood itself! Talk with your friends about how you can secure wood using the material alone. What could you make without using glue or nails? How can the wood interlock or fit together? What are the advantages and disadvantages of securing wood in this way?

MAKE IT!
CRAFT STICK STRUCTURE

Follow these instructions to create a craft stick box—or use these guidelines as inspiration for your own design.

- Plan your design.
- Draw a template based on the length of the craft sticks. Create a square design as a starting point.
- You could paint your craft sticks now, if you prefer. It is easier than painting them after your model is made.

2
- Lay two craft sticks horizontally. Then glue six sticks at right angles to the first two. This forms the base.
- Glue two sticks horizontally on top of your base. Line them up with the first two horizontal sticks. Next, glue two sticks on the left and right, above the outside pair of vertical sticks. Continue to build up layers of sticks. Use different colors if you like.

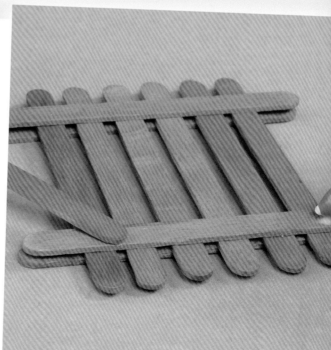

3

- Continue building up your layers using dots of glue to hold everything in position until you have reached your desired height.
- After 20 layers or so, glue craft sticks all around the inside **perimeter** of your box. Leave part of the uprights showing, so the lid will fit securely.

4

- Make a lid using the template you used to make your box. Lay six sticks on your template, and then glue two sticks at right angles along each side. Continue with the layers and dots of glue until you have a top that fits over the vertical sticks of your box.
- If you have used plain sticks, you can decorate them now.

CONCLUSION

Craft sticks are narrow but strong. What does this suggest about why wood is so useful for construction?

Make It Even Better!

Reflect on how you can develop this project. Can you add onto this structure, or create a more detailed and complex model? Work with your friends to design and create other models. Talk together about any useful changes you can make.

FROM TREE TO TIMBER

Some trees are grown in special forests specifically for use as timber. These trees are cut down and turned into planks. This is the wood sold in your local building supply store.

CUTTING A TREE

To **fell** a large tree, two cuts are made near the base of the tree, one on each side. This helps control the direction in which the tree will fall. Once felled, the branches are removed with a large chainsaw, and the tree is cut into manageable logs. The biggest part of the trunk is cut mainly for construction timber. The logs are transported and taken for processing. They are sorted and cut into pieces for different uses: wood for fuel or timber for construction. Other remains from wood are used to make paper.

These logs are transported on a log loader. They will be processed before being sold.

SEASONING

Felling traditionally takes place in the winter months because trees have less moisture content, or water, in them at that time. During the summer months, trees can contain more than 50 percent water. The water inside a tree combines with other chemicals to produce a sticky liquid called sap. When a tree is cut, the cut wood stops growing but the water remains inside. As the water slowly evaporates, or dries up, the cells in the wood shrink. Cut wood needs to have the excess moisture removed, otherwise it will shrink and may rot. Seasoning, or drying, wood is the process of removing excess moisture. Before wood is seasoned, it is known as green wood. If you try to carve or cut green wood, it will shrink and crack.

Wood contains a lot of moisture, so it is stacked up to dry out before it is used in woodwork.

Be a Maker!

Get together with a group of friends and go outdoors to collect some sticks and branches that have fallen naturally. Discuss why you think it is important not to damage or cut healthy trees. Stack your branches and sticks slightly off the ground. Place them in a sunny and windy position, if possible. Cut and carve similar-sized pieces after different periods of time. Record the differences in your results, and discuss them as a group. How does the moisture content affect the wood? Why do you think it affects it in that way?

RECYCLE, REWORK

Brazilian rosewood trees have a strong scent of rose and their wood is strong and heavy, but the species is under threat from **illegal logging**. Too many trees have been cut down. Today, many countries will not allow rosewood or wood from other threatened trees to be taken from one country to another, either as timber or as a finished product.

WASTE WOOD?

Wood is a **renewable resource** only if new trees are planted to replace those that are cut down. There is no such thing as waste wood! It can be used as fuel, or it can be recycled and reworked.

GROW THAT WOOD

Trees absorb the **greenhouse gas** carbon dioxide. When trees are felled to clear land to grow crops, but are not replaced, the result is an excess of carbon dioxide in the atmosphere. Within trees, carbon dioxide is converted to other carbon substances the tree can use, then stored in the wood. Half of the dry weight of wood is carbon. Trees can store carbon for generations without releasing it.

These old wooden picture frames could be used for many different recycling projects. What would you make?

SOURCE IT!

Source wood for your projects from thrift stores. You may spot a wooden picture frame to sand down, paint, and use to frame your own work of art. Or you may want to recycle the wood. Cut it into strips (or carefully detach any screws or nails) and use these pieces of wood in a new creation. Wooden crates or containers are perfect for providing regular-sized timber. As a maker, you will want to source your wood from recycled items. You can also encourage others to buy only from **sustainable** forests, where new trees are planted to replace those cut down. You can share ideas with your friends about where to source wood from and where to find recycled wood.

Arvind Gupta demonstrates some of the simple, but educational, toys he creates from wood.

Makers and Shakers

Arvind Gupta

Arvind Gupta (born 1953) makes science and math fun. He recycles trash, often wood, to inspire a love of learning and an understanding of math and science. The Indian-born scientist shows true maker spirit. After training as an engineer and working in business, he decided to design toys and games for children in poor, rural areas of India, using materials on hand. Check out some of his creations on the Internet.

MAKE IT!
SIGN UP!

How do you know which way to turn when you are walking or driving? Directional signs, of course! Try making your own directional sign. It could give directions to your school, for example. If you are holding a maker event with your friends, you could direct the arrows toward different activities in your event. Be creative. How about directing toward the locations of future maker faires, and add in information about when they take place? What a great way to publicize the creativity of the maker movement!

1
- Plan your design.
- Cut your wood to size for the vertical pole. Sand any rough edges.

2
- Measure your wood for the sign sections. Saw off the edges and sand any rough ends.

3

- Use some wood glue to attach the signs to the pole, then secure it in place with a few wood tacks.
- Use some wood glue to attach your base to the pole, then secure it in place with a few wood tacks.

- Decorate the sign and add the wording.

4

CONCLUSION

Do you need to adjust the angle of the sign sections to accommodate the number of places they point toward? Are the arrows pointing accurately? Are the arrows fixed securely and will they withstand different weather conditions? Discuss with friends ways to make the wood even stronger.

Make It Even Better!

How can you improve the function of your sign? Can you create an activity, such as a puzzle or treasure trail, in which people follow signs to get from one station to another?

HOME SWEET HOME

Scientists and engineers have created incredible **artificial** materials for construction, but many people prefer to build with wood. Wood is an ideal construction material. It is inexpensive, strong, and readily available in most parts of the world.

LOG CABINS

Early settlers in wilderness areas used logs to build houses. After clearing an area of trees, the settlers searched for straight logs. After stripping off the bark, they cut notches at the ends of the logs so they could fit together. They built the four walls in layers, one log at a time. The roof was made from logs with a layer of soil on top. When the walls were in place, the settlers used mud or clay to seal the cracks between the logs.

Think about what you would need to do to make a log cabin like the early settlers did.

Makers and Shakers

Austin Hay

Young American maker Austin Hay (born 1998) had always wanted a tree house. He took his dream into his own hands and developed the concept. Not content with creating a tree house, the 16-year-old decided to build a house on the ground. In true maker spirit, Austin used recycled materials. The space is small, but he designed it with vision and ideas. He even built the house on wheels, so he could move around. As Austin says: "My favorite part of my house is that it is mine and has my blood, sweat, and hard work put into it… I learned a lot on the way."

TAKE SHELTER

You may not be ready to build your own home or tree house, but you can design and build a shelter. Plan it as a joint project with friends. What do you need to consider? Where is your site? Take into consideration the weather and the soil. What kind of wood will you choose and why? Before any construction project, you need to plan. Talk about your ideas, and sketch them out. Draw the frame, then consider possible practical issues and difficulties. Being a maker is about problem-solving: If something is not working, revise your ideas. Ask others and listen to their ideas. Working as a team will produce better and quicker results.

Whenever you build a wooden structure, you must get a responsible adult to check that it is safe for use.

FLOAT THE BOAT

Wood floats. From dugout canoes to massive ships, wood is a perfect material for riding the choppy waves. However, when you are near water, you must take care. If you make a raft or any other kind of boat and float it on water, you must wear a life jacket. Currents can be unpredictable. Until you have tested your craft for safety, you will not know how well it floats with you or others inside.

However well constructed a raft or ship is, it is subject to the challenges of unpredictable waves and weather.

FOLLOWING HISTORY

In 1947, Thor Heyerdahl and a crew of five sailed thousands of miles on a wooden raft from the coast of Peru to Polynesia. The voyage of the *Kon-Tiki*, as the raft was called, took nearly three and a half months. The aim of the journey was to show that the people of South America could have sailed across the Pacific Ocean and settled on the islands of Polynesia.

Fast forward to 2016, and Norwegian Torgeir Higraff and a crew of 13 recreated the journey on wooden rafts. Torgeir needed 44 trees, and he selected them from Ecuador. A team of 30 people built the rafts in three weeks. The crew hoped to bring attention to the effects of **climate change**, but unfortunately they had to abandon their journey due to unexpected weather conditions.

NEW PURPOSE

Makers like to repurpose or recycle whenever they can. Ask friends if they know of anyone who will give you an old boat. Look at the shape of the old boat. Discuss with friends ways to recycle the boat and its wood. Could it become a plant container? Check that there are some holes in the base for good water drainage, and fill the bottom of the boat with soil. A coat of paint on the outside, and colorful plants will complete the transformation. Or you could turn your old boat into a stall at a maker faire to inspire other makers.

Have fun constructing a model boat or raft that is able to carry a load without tipping over!

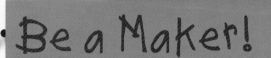

Be a Maker!

It takes a lot of experience to build a raft that is safe for use. Experiment with a toy raft to test the properties of wood. Get together with a group of friends to plan and build a raft. Once you have built your raft, test it in the water. Try it without a load, then with a load. Does it stay balanced? Why not make several rafts and add sails? Have a contest to see which one travels the farthest, then discuss why.

PLAY IT, SHAPE IT

The color, feel, smell, and shape of wood make it special. In everything from toys to sculptures, wood has a beauty that makes it stand out from other materials. Wood can be used for so many different purposes. Armed with whirring chainsaws or hand-carving tools, sculptors create beautiful wooden artworks. Some sculptors work directly with trees. Others work with small pieces of wood. Team up with your friends to make board games or wooden puzzles.

GAME COMPONENTS

Which games do you and your friends like to play? Make a wooden die. Carve it from a piece of wood, or cut and glue together small pieces to form a cube. Shape a piece of wood to make a board for a game. Decide with your friends how to use the die and board to create a new game.

Carving wood with a chainsaw is spectacular, but can be very dangerous. Leave it to the experts!

PUZZLES

You could make a wooden puzzle. They make perfect gifts and keep everyone's brain alert. Take a piece of wood and paint one side of it. That will make it obvious which way up the pieces must go when the player puts the puzzle back together. Draw an image on the nonpainted side of the board. Keep the design simple—straight lines will be easier to cut. Mark the puzzle shapes with a thick pen, then use a knife or scissors to **score** along the marks. With a coping saw, cut out the shapes. You may need to sand down your puzzle to ensure there are no splinters or sharp edges. You may also want to make a box for storing your puzzle pieces.

Complicated puzzles with many curves are cut out using special tools such as a jigsaw or a scroll saw.

Makers and Shakers

Gabriella and Talia Arovas

Two young New York City sisters, Gabriella (born 2005) and Talia Arovas (born 2008), dreamed of new toys. Their parents did not buy them, so in true maker style, the sisters made their own! Gabriella made a piano for her doll, and Talia carved out high-heeled shoes! Both girls shared their skills and creativity at a maker faire, a space where makers come together to inspire and support each other.

MAKING MUSIC

Whether the drum is a log or a pot, a stick or a wooden spoon makes a great drumstick. Wood is a good choice for many musical instruments, because it has a sound quality. It is flexible and quite easy to shape (think of the curve of a guitar), it lasts for a long time—and it even looks good. Blow, pluck, hit—simply listen to the sound of wood.

TYPES OF WOOD

Different types of wood are used to make instruments. Selecting which wood to use is an art in itself. Soft maple is used for its flexibility. This makes it easier to make the curved surfaces of a guitar. Spruce is prized for its tone. Traditionally, ebony and rosewood are used for the **fingerboard** of a violin, maple for the **bridge**, and spruce for the **soundboard**.

A gouge allows you to hollow out a piece of wood one shaving at a time, so the final shape can be very precise.

THE SOUND OF WOOD

The didgeridoo is a traditional **Aboriginal** instrument from Australia. It is usually made from a eucalyptus log that has been hollowed out by termites. First, a tree is tapped to see if it is hollow. Once a hollow tree is found, it is felled and trimmed. The log is thumped on the ground to clear it of termites! A mouthpiece is added and the didgeridoo is then carved or painted. A didgeridoo echoes with the sounds of the natural world, from the wind to flowing water.

A player's breath and the vibration of their lips create the deep sound of the didgeridoo.

Be a Maker!

Look on the Internet at some penny whistles and flutes. What principles can you apply to making your own simple instrument from a stick or branch? Think about what other instruments you can devise from wood that you could use air to play. Try to buy or find a music box. As a special gift, make a new wooden box from recycled wood or reuse an old box as a new casing for your music box. How will you ensure that you can reach the **mechanism** of the original music box to start it playing?

MAKE IT!
BIRDHOUSE

Use your skills to build a birdhouse. Try to source recycled material wherever possible, or **adapt** the pieces if you are reusing an old box. This is a great project to work on as a team, so try to get a group of friends involved. You could also work with some members of your family.

YOU WILL NEED
- Pieces of plywood for the box
- Bamboo garden stake
- Hacksaw and hole saw
- Hammer
- Wood glue, nails, and screws
- Water-based latex paint
- Sandpaper

- Plan your design.
- Cut six pieces of wood to make the box. Sand any rough edges.
- Draw a circle 1¼ inches (3 cm) in diameter on the front section, 1 inch (2.5 cm) from the top. Use a hole saw to cut out the hole. Sand rough edges.
- Assemble the sides and base. Secure them with wood glue.

1

2

- Hammer in nails to secure the wood on the front, back, and base.
- Paint the outside of the box with water-based latex paint to protect the box and the birds that use it. Neutral colors such as grays and browns work best.

28

- Cut lengths of a bamboo garden stake to decorate the roof and glue them into position. Leave a space so the lid can be screwed down. The roof can then be removed so the box can be cleaned at the end of the season.

3

- Screw the lid into position and drop the last cane into place. Do not glue it down.

4

CONCLUSION

Before you put up your birdhouse, look at it and see if you want or need to make changes. Are there improvements you could make to its appearance or the way it works? Ask your family or friends for their opinions.

Make It Even Better!

Different species of birds prefer different birdhouse designs. Research what kind of birds are in your neighborhood. Then use this website to help decide the best dimensions for a birdhouse that will attract those birds: www.birdwatching-bliss.com/ bird-house-dimensions.html

GLOSSARY

Aboriginal Describing people who are native to a country

adapt Make changes to

artificial Made by humans

bridge A piece of wood that raises the strings in a musical instrument

carpentry Making or repairing things in wood

cells Small structures that make up wood and other living things

claw hammer A tool used to drive nails into wood and remove nails from wood

climate change The global change in Earth's weather

conduct Allow something to pass through

coniferous Referring to trees that keep their leaves or needles all year round, also known as evergreens

construction The process of building a structure

deciduous Referring to trees that drop their leaves each year

denser Heavier or more tightly packed

DIY Do-it-yourself

fell Cut down

fingerboard The part of a musical instrument against which the musician's fingers press the strings

functional For practical use

grain Pattern of fibers in wood

greenhouse gas A gas in the air that increases the temperature on Earth

hardwood A hard type of wood that comes from deciduous trees

illegal logging Cutting down trees without permission

insulator A material that keeps heat in or out

mechanism A mechanical part or group of parts that make something work

knots an imperfection in wood where a branch was connected to a tree

perimeter The inside or outside edge of a surface

properties Characteristics and qualities of a material

recycled Reused

renewable resource Natural supply that can grow again, or be used again

score To scratch a line into a surface

softwood Wood that comes from coniferous trees, and is soft and easy to cut

soundboard Part of a string instrument that increases the sound of the strings

sustainable Able to be kept in the same state

timber Pieces of wood cut for use in construction or carpentry

versatile Easy to use in a variety of ways

LEARNING MORE

BOOKS

Felix, Rebecca. *Fun & Creative Workshop Activities: Cool Woodworking Projects* (Cool Industrial Arts). Checkerboard Library, 2016.

Llimós, Anna. *Earth-Friendly Wood Crafts in 5 Easy Steps*. Enslow Elementary, 2014.

The Editors of Make:. Like the Pioneers (Make:). Maker Media, Inc, 2015.

McGuire, Kevin. *The All-New Woodworking for Kids*. Paw Prints, 2008.

WEBSITES

Find some projects to engage your maker skills at:
www.thesawguy.com/woodworking-projects-for-kids

Find links to fun and easy woodworking projects here:
www.instructables.com/id/Woodworking-Projects-for-Beginners

A good start for woodworking projects is:
http://woodprojectsforkids.org

INDEX